MONEY ON

The ABCD's Of Wealth Accumulation

Gavin Taylor

Acknowledgements

Special thanks to Ebun Hill and Latoya Hawkins for doing an amazing job of creating the front and back covers of this book and for your efforts in helping me promote this work. You guys did an amazing job and I am extremely grateful for your hard work and dedication to this project. Special thanks to Bettye Blackston for taking the time to edit this project. I will never forget your labor of love. Special thanks to my mom, Faye Taylor, for encouraging me, during our morning chats, to complete this book. I'm grateful for your love. Now it's your turn to complete the book that God gave you to write. Don't stop until it's completed. I want to give a very special thanks to my amazing and incredible life partner, my beautiful wife, Reverend Tanya Taylor. Thank you for pushing me to complete this book and for being my greatest cheerleader. I love you with all of my heart. Finally, I want to thank my Lord and Savior, Jesus Christ, who gave me the grace and wisdom to write this project. I'm so grateful to you for saving me and for loving me unconditionally.

To: _Amanda_

It is my sincerest hope that this book will be your personal road map to financial independence. I personally believe that if you follow the principles laid out in this book, you will find the financial success that you've been searching for. Don't just read this book; apply the principles written in this book. You've taken the first step, now it's time to see it all the way through until the end. I wish you success as you begin your journey towards financial freedom.

May God Richly Bless You,

Gavin Taylor

Table of Contents

Introduction   **1**

    The Psychology of Money   1

    My Story   4

    Fast Forward to My Mid 20's   5

    How to Read This Book   7

Chapter 1 – "A" is for Asset Accumulation   **8**

    What is an Asset?   8

    Is it an Asset or is it a Liability?   9

    The Key to Acquiring Wealth   12

    Life Insurance is an Asset That
    Your Family Should Never Be Without   14

    Life Insurance Builds an Immediate
    Estate for Your Family   15

    How Much Life
    Insurance Should You Have?   17

    The Difference
    Between Insurance Coverage's   19

    Whole Life Insurance   19

    Term Life Insurance   20

What Type of Life Insurance
Should You Purchase?   21

Retirement Savings is an
Asset for Your Future   24

What is a 401(k) Plan?   26

IRA's   27

Mutual Funds   29

Risk Tolerance in Investing   30

How Do I Make Money in
Mutual Funds?   32

How Do I Acquire Assets
Without Money?   33

Increase Your Ability to Earn   34

Net Worth Worksheet   36

Chapter 2 – "B" is for Budgeting   **38**

Creating a Budget –
Your Key to Financial Freedom   38

Budgets Require Discipline   40

Don't Live Beyond Your Means   41

Setting Your Financial Goals
and Sticking to it   43

Financial Goals Worksheet   46

List All of Your Income Sources   48

Tracking Your Spending Habit   49

Daily Expenses Tracker   52

List Your Expenses   53

Your First Budget Entry: Yourself   55

How Much Should You Pay Yourself?   56

Start an Emergency Fund Account   57

How Much Do I Need In
My Emergency Fund?   58

Continue Saving and
Invest in Your Future   60

Seven Streams of Income   61

Household Budgeting Worksheet   64

Begin to Eliminate any
Unnecessary Expenses   67

What if I Really Do Need More Money?   68

"B" is also for Banking   70

The Envelope System   72

Balance Your Account by
Knowing When Your Payments are Due   73

Bill Paying Worksheet   75

Chapter 3 – "C" is for Credit   **77**

What is Credit?   77

More Valuable than Money?   77

Know and Protect Your Credit   79

Credit is Good, Debt is Bad   80

The Credit Trap   82

How I Fell into Credit Trap   83

Building Your Credit Score   85

What is a Good or Bad Credit Score?   86

How are FICO Scores Calculated?   88

Payment History   88

Account Balance   90

Length of Credit History   91

New Credit Accounts and
Credit Inquiries   92

Mix of Credit Accounts   93

Be Aware of what's
On Your Credit File   95

Getting a Copy of My Credit Report   96

How to Read Your Credit Report   98

Identifying Information   98

Credit History   99

Public Records   100

Inquiries   101

The Misconception of Hard Pulls   103

What type of information will
show up on your Credit Report   104

What type of information
WON'T show up on your Credit Report   104

Corrections Errors Found
on Your Credit Reports   105

Repairing your Credit   107

Get any agreement in writing   108

How to Establish and
Re-establish Your Credit   109

Use an old Credit Card   111

Make Payment on Time   111

Never Max Our Your Credit Cards   112

Make the Collection Accounts a Priority   113

Before Your Pay a Collection Agency   113

Take Out a Personal Loan   115

Use, Don't Abuse, Your Credit Cards   115

Request a credit line increase   117

Never Close Credit Accounts   117

Once you've built your credit,
begin to use it to your advantage   118

Chapter 4 – "D" is for Debt Elimination   **120**

Start the Debt Snowball rolling   121

Other Strategies for Paying Off Debt   123

The Power of Splitting your Payments   123

Apply your Raises to your
Debt or Savings   124

Consider Financial Counseling   126

Introduction

The Psychology of Money

Before we can talk about how you can earn, save, and invest money, we have to deal with your thoughts and attitudes concerning money itself. For most people, their problem is not the lack of money it's their handling of the money that they currently have. It is also important for you to understand the fact that the way you currently manage your money is directly related to what you were taught about money as you were growing up as a child. The sad reality is that most of us were not taught how to handle money. We were taught how to earn money and how to spend money, but most of us were not taught how to handle money or maybe I should say, handle money "properly".

I mean, most of us have grown up in the microwave, fast food, "I want it now" generation. There is no such thing as waiting. Think about it; we become infuriated when the internet is moving slow. We become agitated and frustrated when we're waiting on line. Why? Because, we want it, when we want it and we want it now! Believe it, or not, this type of attitude even trickles down to the way that we handle our money. How, you ask? Well, you may realize that you can't afford that big screen HD TV, but you want it now; so, you charge it on your credit card, and pay three times what it's worth (when you add the interest). Why? Because that credit card told you, "Use me, and you can have what you want now". You don't have to wait until later. You can have it right now and you, just like me, and a lot of other people out there, constantly fall into this trap. You bought it and enjoyed it, until you started paying for it. Now, that big screen TV that you thought was a great deal at $1000.00, after finance charges (interest), cost you $3000.00. Doesn't seem like such a good deal anymore, does? Well that's the way the system is set up.

Didn't you know that credit card companies have increased their efforts to get you, and keep you, in debt? You don't think so? Well how many credit card offers have you received this week? I rest my case. Bottom line, debt is not your friend, and in order to become financially independent, we have to start making better financial decisions. The bible says that, "He becometh poor that dealeth with a slack (lazy or negligent) hand: but the hand of the diligent maketh rich"(Proverbs 10:4). Notice the scripture says that he became poor. That person wasn't poor until he/she became negligent with the handling of his/her finances. Then, as a result of his/her poor money management, he/she became poor. The world puts it like this, "A fool, and his/her money, is soon parted".

So what's the solution? The solution is, we have to stop being foolish and negligent with our finances and start making wise financial decisions. That will only happen, when we get sick and tired of being in debt and broke. Bottom line, in order to change, you have to be mad at your situation. You have to become so angry at being in debt, being broke and being in financial distress, that you're willing to make some changes.

You may have had a bad habit of mishandling finances. Now, you're going to have to change your habit, and that's going to take discipline. As you're reading this book, you're going to need two things in order to succeed. 1). You're going to need accurate information and 2). You're going to need discipline. The first one is the reason this book was created. The second will be up to you. I can only give you information, but I can't make you do it. However, if you will apply these principles, that I am going to teach you, you will never regret it. You will wake up, be debt free, and financially secure. Now, it won't happen over night. This is not a "Get rich quick scheme". It's a lifestyle that will lead you to financial freedom. That's were the discipline comes in.

My Story

My financial story began when I first entered into college as a freshman. Just like many other young men, I couldn't wait to climb from underneath the confines of a strict parent and start living on my own. So, I jumped at the chance to stay at my college dorm. For me, it was as if I had been paroled. I was free. I could do my own thing. Nobody could tell me what time I needed to be in the house. I could stay out as long as I like. I'm sure that some of you have been there.

However, after the novelty of being "free" wore off, I began to realize that it cost money to be on your own. I hated the cafeteria food that meant that I had to buy food. I needed clothes, but clothes cost money. I needed to get around, but it cost money to drive a car. I did manage, however, to secure a decent work-study job on campus. It paid slightly higher than minimum wage, but that money was supposed to be going towards paying the tuition that my loans didn't cover, but I found myself using the money to pay for everyday expenses. I must say, I was really struggling financially. That's when I discovered credit.

Yes, I was one of those unfortunate youngsters that received the credit card offer and dove in head first. I don't want to make a long story longer, so let me just say this. I wound up taking out multiple credit cards, a car note and a personal loan, without a real plan to pay it off. I'm ashamed to say that I fell into the credit trap and I destroyed my credit for many years.

Fast forward to my mid 20's

After many years of struggling with bad credit, I made a decision that I didn't want to struggle any more. I remember praying and asking God to help me get out of this financial mess that I put myself in. It was at that time that I began to research all of the information that I could find on building credit and becoming financially independent. I will admit, I didn't climb out of the financial gutter overnight. It took some years to clean up the mess that I placed myself in; but, with information and discipline, I was able to pull myself out.

After I pulled myself out, I decided that I wanted to help others do the same. So, I have spent the last 20+ years of my life doing exactly that. In fact, that is the reason why I wrote this book. The information contained in this book is the information that I gathered over the last 20 years working in finance. This is the information that I wish I had when I was a teenager. This is the information that I used to dig myself out of the gutter and I believe that you can use it to do the same. This book is not meant for the savvy investor or for the person that already has their finances in order. This book was written specifically for those that want to learn how to become debt free and financially independent. I hope that you enjoy this book and that you use it to achieve financial independence.

How to Read this Book

There are four primary sections to this book. That's why I call it the "The ABCD's of Wealth Accumulation". As you read this book, you will find out that some of you may desperately need the information in all of the chapters, while others may only need the information from a couple of the sections. The first section deals with Asset Accumulation. In this section, we will discuss the difference between assets and liabilities. We also discuss how to accumulate assets. The second section deals with the concept of Budgeting. It is my belief that you will never achieve financial independence if you don't have control of your money and your spending habits. This section discusses how to put together a budget for your finances. The third section is the Credit section. In my experience, more people have issues with this than anything else. In fact, the vast majority of my work is with people that are trying to repair and rebuild their credit. This section was created for that purpose. Finally, the fourth section is for Debt Elimination. In this section, I concentrate on tools and techniques for paying down and paying off debt. There you have it, the ABCD's (Asset, Budget, Credit and Debt) of Wealth Accumulation. Let's start our journey towards financial freedom. Hope you enjoy the ride.

CHAPTER 1

"A" is for Asset Accumulation

What is an Asset?

As we begin our discussion on "The ABCD's Wealth Accumulation", the "A" stands for Asset Accumulation; but before we can discuss how to accumulate assets, we must first discuss what an asset is. The technical definition of an asset is "a useful or valuable thing, person or quality". It is also defined as "property owned by a person or company, regarding as having value and available to meet debts, commitments, or legacies". That's the standard Google dictionary definition of an asset. Now, the "MONEY ON MY STREET" definition for an asset is simply something that puts money into your pocket. That makes sense, right?

Therefore, if it can put money into your pocket, it is considered an asset. For example, you can consider your job an asset. Why? Because every pay period it deposits money into your bank account. It is, therefore, a valuable asset to you, because it puts money into your pocket on a regular basis. With that being said, as long as it is something that is making deposits and not withdrawals, we are going to consider it to be an asset to you. It doesn't matter how often the money is deposited, what's important is that (whatever it is) it's putting money in your pocket and not removing it from your pocket.

Is it an Asset or is it a Liability?

Now, we can't speak about assets, without also discussing the concept of liabilities. So, if our definition for an asset is something that puts money into your pocket, then a liability is something that removes money from your pocket. With that being said, we must be careful to not confuse an asset with a liability, which most people often tend to do. For example, if you were to ask most people what their greatest asset was, they would probably say either their house or their car, but that may or may not be true. Your home actually could be an asset or a liability. It depends on the use of that house. If you and your family are the only ones that live in that house, then your house is not an asset to you, it's a liability. Why? Because it doesn't put money in your pocket every month, it takes money out of your pocket every month.

Think about it. You have to pay a mortgage on that house. You have to pay interest on that house. You have to pay taxes on that house. You have to pay insurance on the house. You also have to pay a water bill, electric, gas, and (if something breaks or deteriorates) you have to pay to repair that house. All of these expenses take money out of your pocket every month. That is not an asset, it's a liability.

Now, if you own a multi-family home (e.g. a 2, 3 or 4 family home) and you rent out the other apartments and you use the rent from those apartments to pay for the mortgage, interest, taxes and insurance, while you live rent free, then it's considered an asset. Why? Because, instead of the home taking money out of your pocket every month, it actually deposits money into your pocket every month.

As I mentioned, people sometimes also (mistakenly) confuse their cars for assets. But, just like a house, it could be an asset or a liability. If your car is only used for your personal use, then it is not an asset, it's a liability. Why? Because, the moment that you drove that brand spanking new beauty off the lot, it began to decrease in value. If you tried to sell it the same day that you bought it, it wouldn't be worth as much as you paid for it. Also, if you financed or leased that car, it's costing you a monthly car payment. You also have to pay for gas, insurance and continued upkeep on that car. Therefore, it is a liability, because it is constantly taking money out of your pocket on a regular basis.

Now, I personally have a side used car business. I go to auctions, purchase cars at a discount and sell them for more than what I purchased them for. The cars that I buy and sell are assets to me, as long as I can sell them for more than what I purchased them for. Also, if you use your car to earn an income, like when you drive Uber or Lyft, your car may also be considered an asset to you. If you're making enough money, through Uber or Lyft, to pay your car note, insurance, gas and make some money to put into your pocket, your car is now an asset.

Hope that clarifies the difference between assets and liabilities. Now you can apply this logic to any other endeavor that you participate in and determine whether or not you have an asset or a liability. Why is this information important to you? It's important because the key to financial freedom is in accumulating more assets than liabilities. In other words, you have to invest in more things that will put money in your pockets (assets) and invest less money in things that will take money out of your pocket (liabilities).

The Key to Acquiring Wealth

The number one way that you can start the process of building your personal wealth and accumulating assets is by starting with what you already have. If you want to start acquiring assets, it would be wise to start by tapping into your first asset; your current personal income. Remember that I mentioned (earlier) that your job was an asset to you? It's an asset, because it puts money into your pocket every pay period. So, why not use that income to build wealth and secure additional assets that can put more money into your pocket?

I personally believe that it is very sad to see someone work a job all year long and all they have to show for it is that they paid bills and living expenses. Most people don't have anything to show for working hard all year long. This is not living life; it's existing. Far too many people are going through life living paycheck to paycheck. If the average person lost their job, today or tomorrow, they would be in a desperate situation. This is also why so many people are not retiring comfortably. They have never developed a healthy savings mentality. They are just working to get by and to maintain their current standard of living. People have to start understanding that the government is not going to take care of them. Social Security may not even be around when you retire. If it is around, people will find out (the hard way) that it will not provide enough income to allow them to maintain the same type of lifestyle that they were accustomed to living, prior to retirement.

People are also going to have to realize that companies don't take care of their employees like they used to. Companies are now placing the burden of retirement planning on their employees. Therefore, in order for you to have a happy retirement, you have to start planning for it. Bottom line, if you're not saving for retirement, you will not be retiring. With all that being said, you have to start using your current income to start building wealth and accumulating assets. We will discuss this in more detail in the Budget section.

Life Insurance is an Asset that your family should never be without…

Before we discuss other types of assets, I want to discuss an asset that most people usually don't even consider. That's right; Life Insurance. It may not be an asset to you, because it doesn't put any money in your pocket, but in the unfortunate event that you pass prematurely, it will be a huge asset to your loved ones. The fact of life is that all people (eventually) have to die. Some people will die sooner and some later, but no one can escape this inevitability.

The purpose of a life insurance policy is to make sure that you take care of the loved ones that you'll be leaving behind. Just like you would protect your spouse and/or children from something that's trying to harm them in life, insurance is a way of protecting them from the dangers of financial strains after you've passed on. I don't know about you, but I have attended far too many funerals of individuals that passed on without having insurance coverage. Death without insurance is an incredible financial burden on an already grieving family.

The average funeral cost is approximately $10,000. That's not an easy amount for most families to come up with at a moment's notice. So, what does the family do in this case? Usually, they have to contact every family member and try to raise this astronomical amount of money for the funeral. When that doesn't work, I've seen many people turn to social media sites (e.g. Go Fund Me and Facebook), to ask their friends and acquaintances to help them pay for the funeral expenses. Now ask yourself this question. Do you really want to put your family through this type of an ordeal? I mean, they're already grieving over your loss, now they have to suffer with an additional financial burden on top of that. Investing in a life insurance policy removes that extra stress. Now your family can focus on moving on without you, instead of being burdened by you with your final expenses.

Life Insurance Builds an Immediate Estate for your Family...
One of the benefits of having a life insurance policy is that it builds an immediate estate for your family. It's unfortunate, but, most people will pass on without leaving any assets to their family. In order for the next generation to go further (financially) then we did, we must leave them something to get started with. That's how families build generational

wealth. The first generation begins to acquire the assets. They, then, leave those assets to the next generation. Then the next generation's responsibility is to take those assets, that they were left with, and use them to accumulate more assets. And so on and so on and so on. That's how each generation does better than the previous.

When you don't leave anything to the next generation, they have to struggle just as much as you did. Our goal, therefore, should be to leave our children with something to get them started. If you can't, in your lifetime, accumulate assets to leave behind, at least you can leave insurance money behind. Think about this. If you have just enough life insurance to take care of your burial and to insure that your children have enough money to pay for college, how amazing of a head start is that? Now your children can go to school without having to worry about taking out loans for college. That could save them $50,000 to $100,000 in student loan debt.

Now they can graduate college and start to build, instead of graduating college worrying about how they're going to pay off a mountain of student loan debt. That makes life so much easier for them and enables them to start fresh and unencumbered by debt. If they're wise, they will begin to build wealth to enjoy and then leave it to their children. Then the wealth cycle can continue for generations.

How Much Life Insurance Should you have?

How much life insurance someone needs varies person by person. Your personal, unique, situation will determine how much life insurance coverage you're going to need. If you're single, with no dependents, you're not going to need as much insurance as someone that is married with 3 children. So, I'm going to try to make this as simple as possible, to help you determine how much insurance you should have.

You should first factor in the amount that it's going to take to bury yourself. A proper burial costs (approximately) $10,000 for final expenses. That will purchase a pretty nice funeral. Next, you have to calculate your remaining outstanding debt. This is especially important if you have a spouse and/or children that you're leaving behind. The last thing that you want to leave your family with is debt, because the bills don't stop coming because you've passed on. Worst off, now your family doesn't have your income to help pay those bills. So, take some time and calculate your debt and include that in your life insurance amount (we will go over how to obtain this information in the Credit and Debt section).

Next, if you have children, you probably want them to go to college. Like I mentioned earlier, how awesome would it be, even if you weren't around to see it, to be able to pay for your children's college tuition? Research the average amount that it would cost for your kids to go to school for 4 years and factor that cost in. You should be able to Google this information. Make sure to use a calculator that will adjust for inflation, because the cost of college tuition keeps going up.

Finally, you need to understand the fact that the primary use for insurance should be to replace the income that you're not providing any more. You can never be replaced, but your income can. If you take your current salary and multiply it by 10, you can replace your income for the next 10 years for your family. For example, if you're currently making $50,000 per year, a $500,000 life insurance policy will replace your income for 10 years ($50,000 x 10 = $500,000). If your spouse is a wise investor, or consults with a good financial adviser, they may be able to take that lump sum life insurance payment, invest it properly and live off the interest for the rest of their life. That's it!

Now you just add it all up and you have the amount of life insurance that you should have. Now, remember, everyone is different. You may not need to pay for your kid's college tuition, because you might not have any. So, make the adjustments as you see fit. This is just a starting point to help you determine how much insurance you need.

The Difference between Insurance Coverages

Whole Life Insurance

When looking at Life Insurance options, there are two primary types of policies to choose from; Term and Whole Life. There are other variations of policies, such as variable life and universal life and others, but we're going to focus on these two for the purpose of this book. Whole Life Insurance is just what the name indicates. It's a policy that is going to last you your entire (whole) life. It's an insurance that provides both a death benefit and it also allows you to build up cash value within the policy. You can borrow from this cash value, once it accumulates, and use it for whatever you desire. The issue with borrowing, however, is that you must pay the borrowed amount back, with interest, or the borrowed amount will be reduced from the death benefit. For example, if you have a $150,000 Whole Life Insurance policy and you borrow $50,000 from the cash value, you must pay the $50,000 back (with interest) or your death benefit will be reduced to $100,000. Also, with a Whole Life policy, your premium payments end at age 100. At that point, you won't have to pay any more premiums and your death benefit is secure.

Term Life Insurance

Term Life Insurance, on the other hand, does not last you your whole life. It will last you for the set term that you have established. For example, it could be a 20 or 30 or a 35 year term policy. Once the term ends, the policy is over. There is no cash value and you don't get any of your premium payments back. Wait! Before you give up on hearing about this type of policy, you need a little more information. Since Term policies are considered pure coverage, because you're only paying for insurance coverage, they are much cheaper than Whole Life policies. With a Whole Life policy, part of your premium payment goes towards the insurance, while the other portion (of your premium payment) goes towards the cash value. With that being said, the cash value option makes the Whole Life policy much more expensive than the Term Policy option.

What Type of Life Insurance should you purchase?

Most Financial Advisors will advise you that Term Insurance is the best value for your money. They will tell you that the best thing for you to do is buy term insurance and invest the difference, of what you will pay for a Term Life policy, in comparison to what you would pay for a Whole Life policy. But, for the purpose of illustration, let's look at a scenario to explain why Term Insurance is the better option.

If I were to purchase a 30 year Term Policy at age 30, with a Preferred Plus health status (that means that the person is in excellent health), a non-smoker, with a $500,000 death benefit, it would cost me (approximately) $33.00 per month for the coverage.

In order for me to get a Whole Life insurance policy at age 30, with a Preferred Plus health status, a non-smoker, with a $500,000 death benefit, it would cost me (approximately) $442.00 per month (I obtained this information by googling quotes on the internet).

That means that it would cost me $409.00 more to get the Whole Life policy option, than it would if I were to purchase the Term Insurance policy. But, you may be thinking, the insurance coverage is for his whole life, instead of 30 years and he is getting cash value. That's somewhat true, but not completely. While the coverage will last the client for their whole life, the cash value that's being accumulated, never becomes more than the total face value of the policy. In other words, in this scenario, the cash value never becomes more than the $500,000 death benefit.

So, you can either take out the $500,000 cash value, or your family will receive the $500,000 death benefit once you pass away. That's right, you will not receive both. You only receive one or the other. Now, let's look at the Term Life option.

Well, if you took the difference of what you pay for the Term Policy ($33.00 per month) and what you would pay for the Whole Life policy ($442.00 per month) and invested it, you would have $409.00 per month to save and invest for your future. Mind you, you have 30 years to invest this money. So, let's look at that scenario. If you started investing $409.00 per month at age 30, when your Term Life policy starts, and you continued to invest that $409.00 for the length of your 30 year Term Policy, earning an interest rate of 11% (which is the average rate for the Standard & Poor's 500 over the last 30 years), you would have investment savings of (approximately) $937,002. Now, let me ask you, would you rather have a $500,000 Whole Life policy or nearly a million dollars in cash? I'm assuming the million dollars.

Buying the Term Policy enabled you to have this extra money to save. If you were to pass away within the 30 year term, your family would have received the $500,000 death benefit. And, if you outlived the Term Policy, you would have investment savings. You may not have a life insurance policy any more, but do you need it if you have a million dollars? At this point, you are considered to be "Self-Insured". Why? Because the only reason you needed insurance at all, was because you didn't have money. If you have money, you don't need insurance. Now, you have money, so you don't need insurance. That's why the Term Insurance option is the better option. But, it's only the better option, if you will be disciplined enough to invest the difference.

Retirement Savings is an Asset for your Future

Retirement savings is a topic that we all need to address. Why? Because employers do not take care of their employees like they used to. There was a time when you could work with a company for 30 years and then retire with a pension that would take care of you for the rest of your life. Unfortunately, those days are long gone. Most people won't work for their company for 30 years. With downsizing and forced retirement, many employees will not be with their employer for the long haul.

Also, the robust pension plans, that used to exist, have been replaced with retirement plans that depend on the employee to make the bulk of the contributions. Also, don't let me forget to mention social security. I don't know about you, but I'm not sure if it will be around when I retire. It might be around, but do you want to take the risk of depending on it to be there at your retirement? At this point in my life, I see social security as "gravy".

In other words, if I get it, great! That gives me some additional money to retire with, but (again) I'm not counting on it. With all that being said, you have to start thinking about, and saving for your retirement now. You don't have time to waste.

We are witnessing more and more people retiring without adequate savings. You don't believe me? Let me ask you this question, do you think that the little old lady wanted to greet you at Walmart this morning? How about the old man working the toll booth? This is the one that really gets to me, the same lady that crossed me across the street, when I was in 5th grade, is still crossing kids across the street today. I seriously doubt, at her age, that she still wants to do that. So, why do they do it? Necessity!

They don't have enough money to live on, so they have to stay in the workforce. What's worse is that their job probably laid them off or forced them to retire early and hired a younger person for far less money. Meanwhile, in their retirement years, not many jobs want to hire senior workers. Their only option is crossing guard, or Walmart greeter or toll booth attendant. So, you need to start saving for retirement, as soon as possible, so that this won't be your story. So, let's start talking about your retirement savings options.

What is a 401(k) Plan?

Named after section 401(k) of the Internal Revenue Code, a 401(k) is an employer-sponsored retirement plan for employees. If your employer offers a 401(k) plan, you can elect to contribute a portion of your income to be invested into the plan. The best part about a 401(k) plan is that your contributions happen before income taxes are taken out of your paycheck. What that means is that you are not being federally taxed on your full income. In other words, you receive a tax savings while you're contributing to your retirement plan. Taxation only happens after you have reached retirement age and you begin to start withdrawing your funds. The benefit of that is that you're usually in a lower tax bracket at retirement than you are now. Meaning that your tax liability will probably be far less during retirement than it is right now.

If your employer does offer a 401(k) plan, you also want to find out if they will match the money that you contribute. Every company has a different policy, when it comes to matching, so make sure you're aware of your company's policy. For example, some companies will match dollar for dollar of what you contribute, up to a certain percentage. Other companies will match up to 50%. If your company does match your contributions, then you are actually receiving free money (up to 100%) on the contributions that you make. You must, therefore, at least contribute up to the amount that your company will match. In term of investment options, you will usually see mutual funds (discussed a little later), stocks, bonds, etc. The majority of the 401(k) investment options, however, will be mutual funds. Now, let's discuss other retirement options.

IRA's

IRA stands for Individual Retirement Account. It is primarily for individuals that are not offered a retirement plan on their job, but it is also for individuals that want to diversify their savings, even if they have a retirement option on their job. There are two types of IRA's; a Traditional IRA and a Roth IRA.

Traditional IRA contributions are tax deductible on both state and federal income tax returns in the year that you make a contribution to it. When you begin to make withdrawals (in retirement) the distributions are taxed at the ordinary income tax rates. Roth IRA's, on the other hand, don't provide a tax break when you're making contributions, but your earnings and your withdrawals are tax-free when you make withdrawals during retirement. As you can see, (for the most part) the Roth IRA is the more attractive of the two types of IRA's.

With both IRA's, the maximum annual contribution is (currently) $5,500 for individuals ($11,000 for married couples) under the age of 50. However, if you are over the age of 50, you can contribute an additional $1,000 ($6,500 per person or $13,000 per couple) per year. Let me also mention that since an IRA is for the purpose of retirement savings, there is a penalty of 10% if you make withdrawals prior to being 59 ½, unless it's for a qualified expense. The qualified expenses are qualified first-time homebuyer expenses, post-secondary education expenses and medical expenses. You will still be subject to paying taxes on the distribution, but the 10% penalty will be waived.

Roth IRA contributions (but not earnings) can be withdrawn penalty- and tax-free at any time, even before the age of 59 ½. Also, since IRA accounts are set up and controlled by the account owner, investment options are not limited to what is made available by a plan provider. This gives IRA accounts a greater degree of investment flexibility and independence than employees that are investing in their company's 401(k) plan.

Mutual Funds

So, we've looked at 401(k) plans and IRA's as retirement planning options. Now, we have to talk about what types of investments are in those plans. This is how I like to describe retirement savings. The plan, whether it's a 401(k) or an IRA, is the car that's travelling along the long road to retirement. The investments within the 401(k) or the IRA are the drivers that get you there. How fast you make it to retirement will greatly depend on the vehicle you're in (the plan) and the driver of that car (the investment). If one of these two things are not right, you may never make it to your destination (retirement) or it may be a longer drive than necessary.

With that being said, let's talk about the investments. Normally, your 401(k) plan or your IRA (whether Traditional or Roth) will be made up of mostly mutual funds. A mutual fund is a collection of stocks and/or bonds and/or other securities. You can think of a mutual fund as a company that brings together a group of people and invests their pool of money in stocks, bonds, and other securities. Each investor owns shares, which represent a portion of the holdings of the mutual fund.

Risk Tolerance in Investing

When you invest in a 401(k) or an IRA, your "risk tolerance" will determine how slowly or quickly you'll reach your monetary investment goal. Have you ever heard "No risk, no reward"? That is definitely the truth when it comes to investing your money. The more risky you are, the more opportunity you will have to reap higher rewards, but you will also run the risk of losing money. The less risky you are, the less opportunities you'll have to reap higher rewards, but your money will be much safer. The question you must ask yourself is can you stomach potential loss?

If you have a higher risk tolerance, you will have more stocks in your mutual fund portfolio. Stocks are the most risky of all of the investment options. After that, you have bonds. Bonds are a less risky option than stocks. After that you have your cash accounts, which are not very risky at all. What you want to be aware of, however, is that as your risk level goes down, so does your ability to earn higher rates of return on your money. The less risky the investment, the smaller your return will be on your money. The more risky the investment the higher the possibility of securing a higher rates of return.

When I counsel people, regarding investing, I always tell them that your age should determine how risky you should be, not your feelings and emotions. If you're in your 20's, you should not be worrying about losing your money, if you have invested wisely. The market goes up and down, but over the last 30 years, the Standard & Poor's (or S&P) 500 has averaged an 11% rate of return. That includes the down years of the Great Recession (2007-2009).

Therefore, if you have 20 or more years to invest, you want should be more risky in your investment options. Now, if you're coming closer to retirement, you want to start becoming less risky. You should begin to move your money from stocks to bonds and cash, because a loss (in your later years) would be devastating. My advice, therefore, is to find an index fund that mirrors the S&P 500 and invest in that for the long haul.

As you get older (around 50 years old), start moving your money to bonds and cash as you get ready to retire.

How Do I Make Money in Mutual Funds?

There are three primary ways that you can make money in a mutual fund. The first way is that income is earned from dividends on the stocks that you invest in and interest on bonds. A fund pays out nearly all of the income it receives over the year to fund owners in the form of a distribution. This distribution can be reinvested back into the mutual fund to purchase more shares.

Secondly, if the fund sells the securities (within the mutual fund) that have increased in price, the fund has what's considered a "capital gain". Most funds also pass on these gains to investors in a distribution or you can reinvest them back into the mutual fund to purchase more shares.

Finally, if mutual funds holdings increase in price, but are not sold by the fund manager, the fund's shares increase in price. You can then sell your mutual fund shares for a profit. Let me reiterate, however, that since the 401(k) and the IRA is for the purpose of retirement savings, there is a 10% tax and penalty of 10% if you make withdrawals prior to being 59 ½. The goal is not to touch this money until you retire. That's how you will get the most benefit out of both the 401(k) and the IRA retirement savings option.

How Do I Acquire Assets without Money?

This is the million dollar question. How do you get started without money? I know that you've always heard that "you have to have money to make money". In some cases, this a very true statement, but not in all cases. There are multitudes of people that have made money without starting with money. You know what it's called; it's called "Sweat Equity". That's right! Good, old fashioned, hard work. You may not have money right now, but you do have the ability to work. So, start with what you have. You may be saying, "Well, my job only gives me enough money to make ends meet". If that's the case, you may want to look for a secondary job that you can use for savings, becoming debt free and investing for your future. There's so many ways to make a secondary income now a days, that there is not much room to say that you can't. For example, you can drive Uber or Lyft to make an additional income. You can deliver pizzas. You can start a small business, doing something that you already like to do. Bottom line, there are many different ways to make additional income. The key is to locate what you can do to earn it.

Increase Your Ability to Earn

You must always look for ways to increase your ability to earn additional income. Preferably without having to work another 40 hour a week job to do it. So, the question that most people ask me is "how do I increase my ability to earn income"?

There are many ways to go about this, so I will just mention a few. You can go back to school to get a degree or try to acquire an additional degree or you can secure a certification in an area that interests you. I knew that I was interested in financial consulting, so it made sense for me to acquire additional certifications (in the financial field) that would help me become more valuable to my clients and that would help me acquire additional income.

Many years ago, I learned how to do taxes. Then I acquired my Life Insurance Producers license. After that I secured a Series 6 for investments, which enabled me to sell Mutual Fund accounts to my clients. Sometime later I became a certified credit counselor.

As I expand the services that I offer, I am able to better service my clients. As I provide these additional services to my clients, I also increase my ability to make additional income. That's how you begin to increase your ability to earn income. So, now you have to determine what interests you and how you can increase your ability to earn by tapping into it. The key is locating your passion. If you can find a way to earn income by doing something that you're passionate in, it will never feel like work. This passion may become a business that can lead to complete financial freedom for you.

Now that you've reviewed the section on assets, use the following "Net Worth" Statement Worksheet" to determine how many Assets vs Liabilities you have and to determine your current Net Worth.

NET WORTH WORKSHEET

Assets

Cash on hand $_____

Cash in Checking Account(s) $_____

Cash in Savings Account(s) $_____

Money Market Account(s) $_____

Market Value of You Home $_____

Rental Property Income $_____

Estimated Value of Household Items $_____

Market Value of Other Real Estate $_____

Stocks $_____

Bonds $_____

Mutual Funds $_____

Market Value of Vehicles $_____

Current Value of 401(k), 403(b), etc. $_____

Current Value of
Individual Retirement Account $_____

Estimated Value of Personal Items $_____

Other Assets _____ $_____

Value of Current Assets $_____

Liabilities

Mortgage Balance $_____

Home Equity Loan or Line of Credit $_____

Other Real Estate Loan $_____

Auto Loan or Lease $_____

Credit Card Balances $_____

Student Loans $_____

Delinquent Taxes $_____

401(k) or 403(b) Loan $_____

Personal Loan $_____

Other Liabilities $_____

Total Liabilities $_____

TOTAL NETWORTH $_____

(Assets minus Liabilities)

CHAPTER 2

"B" is for Budgeting

Creating a Budget - Your Key to Financial Freedom...

I have heard it said that a budget "Plugs up the holes in a leaky pocketbook." I can tell you, by experience, that this statement is very true. When I was younger, I was very poor at managing and budgeting money. That's probably why I didn't have much of it. I would get paid on Friday, and by Monday I wouldn't know where all of my money went. The problem was the fact that I didn't budget my money. I just got it, and spent it. As fast as it came, it went. Most people live life like this. I have counseled many individuals that have no idea where there money is going or what they are spending their money on.

I remember working with this young man with his finances. He told me that his problem was that he needed to make more money. He told me that he would find himself in a financial hole by the end of every month. After I set up a budget for him, to his amazement, he should have been able to save nearly $800.00 per month, after paying all of his expenses. So, where was all of his money going? He had no idea.

This is what most people will tell you if you ask them. They don't know, because their money is not budgeted. It's earned and then it's spent. That's why I always start with setting up a budget for my clients. We need to answer that question (e.g. Where is your money going?), before we can set up a financial strategy. It always amazes me that, once I assist someone with developing a budget, most people are totally shocked that they actually have money left over, after they pay their bills. That's the purpose and the power of having budget.

It helps us to determine if there is any "Disposable Income" available. This is the money that you have left over, after you have paid all of your bills. This is the money that you're going to use to become debt free. This is the money that you're going to use to build your wealth. Never forget that your income is the most powerful tool that you have to build wealth, so you must regain control of it, and not let it control you.

Budgets Require Discipline

The first thing you have to realize, when you're creating a budget, is that budgets require discipline. You are going to have to discipline yourself to ONLY spend what you have allotted in your budget, and not a penny more. If you have allotted $50.00 a week for pocket money, once that $50.00 is spent (I don't care if you have five days to go until your next check), that's it. You will have to be broke until your next pay check. I'm sorry, but that's the only way that you're budget is going to work efficiently. Bottom line, your budget is only as good as you are disciplined to follow it. Otherwise, it's just numbers on a piece of paper.

With that being said, you are going to have to learn how to delay your desires until you can actually afford them. We are all, unfortunately, burdened with more desires than we can afford. We all have things that we don't necessarily need, but we just want. We must begin to view these unnecessary items for what they really are; a waste of money. This, however, is not an easy thing to do. If it was, then it wouldn't require discipline.

The question then becomes, how do I discipline myself to handle money properly and stick to my budget? I'll say this much, the first month is the hardest. If you can "survive" the first month, it will get easier and easier to stick to it. Let me also mention this. The more your savings increase and your debt decreases, the more encouraged you will be to continue. Also, scientifically speaking, if you can last the first month (or 30 days), you will have created yourself a new habit. Once savings and debt reduction and budgeting becomes a habit, you will do it as a matter of second nature.

Don't Live Beyond Your Means

The next issue you have to tackle is that you can't live beyond your means. In other words, if you want to stay on budget, you can't spend more money than you make. That means, as I mentioned earlier, that you have to forgo the items that are "wants" and only buy the things that you actually need. You may "want" a new pair of shoes, but they may not be something that you need. You may "want" a new TV, but that may not be something that you need. You need a place to live. You need food to eat. The bottom line is you can't confuse your "needs" with your "wants".

"Wants" are budget busters. "Wants" will keep you in debt. "Wants" will cause you to spend money that you don't have.

Now, if you really want that new TV, save for it. Allot money, from your budget, for luxury items. It may take you 6 months to save for it, but at least you didn't go into debt to get it. I don't want you to feel like you can't have the things that you want. You can have some luxury items. What I am saying, is that I don't want you to go into debt to buy things that you just "want", but don't really "need". So, stay within your means. Staying within your means just simply means that you don't spend more money than you make. I know that sounds simple, but the vast majority of people are living way beyond their means. This is how debt begins to creep in on people. Since they can't afford what they want, they go into debt to get it.

Setting Your Financial Goals and Sticking to it

The first step in making a budget is to set some realistic financial goals. Depending on your income and expenses, you may have a simple goal of making sure that you spend less money than you make. You may also have a goal of saving an emergency fund, or saving for retirement, a home down payment, debt reduction or maybe college tuition for your children. Whatever your goals are, make sure that you establish them and that you write them down. Why is this important?

It's important because you must always have a reason why you're doing something. To take that a step further, your "Why" must be stronger than your immediate desires. If your "Why" is not compelling enough, you will fall back into old patterns of behavior. Your "Why" must be worth putting off your immediate wants and desires. That's why it's important to develop a compelling "Why" and why you need to write it down.

You must write it down, so that you can look at it every time you're tempted to fall back into old behavior. Once you write it down, make sure that you put it in a place that you will see it on a regular basis. The refrigerator is always a good place to put it. Some put there "why" statement on their bathroom mirror. Others have begun to utilize their smart phones to take care of this task. You can put it in your phone notes. You can also set up a reminder, on your smart phone that sends you an email on a daily basis. For example, one of my goals was to write a little bit of this book (that you're reading right now) every day. I set up a daily reminder in my Google calendar to remind me to write every day.

If your goal is to save for a home, make sure that you set a long term goal that has the final number in mind. For example, you may want to save $25,000 for a down payment. That's the long term goal. The next question that you need to ask is, how much time are you giving yourself to save this amount of money? Let's say your goal is three years. That means that you would have 36 months to save this amount, which means that you have to save $695.00 per month to reach this goal. That's your short term goal. Now you have to figure out a way to free up this amount on a monthly basis, so you can reach this goal. That's where your budget comes into play.

To help you set your financial goals, please feel free to use the "Financial Goals Worksheet" on the following page. Use this sheet to create your "SMART" goals. SMART stands for Specific, Measureable, Achievable, Realistic and Timely. Specific means, what is your goal. Is it to purchase a home or to pay for your kid's college tuition? Whatever it is, write a specific goal down.

Next, your goal must be Measureable. In other words, if your goal is to save for a down payment, how much is that down payment? Next we come to Achievable. In other words, is this a realistic goal in the time that you have allotted for yourself? If you don't have any money saved, you may not be able to purchase a home six months from now. This leads to the next area, which is being Realistic. Is your goal doable? Is it possible for you to accomplish, especially in the time that you've allotted for yourself?

Finally, the last letter is for Timely. What is your time frame for completing this goal? Use the following worksheet to complete this exercise. Remember, that your "Why" has to be compelling enough for you to change your habits. So, make it a good one.

Financial Goals Worksheet (SMART)

Use this worksheet to create a "SMART" goal. Identify a goal that is short, mid, and long-term when completing. Make copies of this worksheet for each individual goal.

Start Date: _____   **Date Achieved:** _____

Verify that your goal is SMART

Specific: What is your goal? (What? Why? and How?)

_____

_____

_____

Measureable: How will you measure your progress?
(How Many? How Much?)

_____

_____

_____

Achievable: Is achieving this goal realistic with effort and commitment? What steps are involved?

_____

_____

_____

Financial Goals Worksheet (SMART) (Cont.)

Realistic: What Skills and knowledge are necessary to reach the goal? Is it do-able?

_____

_____

_____

Timely: When will you achieve this goal?

_____

_____

_____

This goal is important because:

_____

_____

_____

_____

_____

_____

_____

_____

_____

List All of Your Income Sources

Now that you've set your financial goals, now you have to create your budget to assist you in reaching your goals. So, the first step to developing a successful budget is to list all of your "Income Streams". As it sounds, an income stream is the valuable asset that causes money to flow into your pockets on a regular basis. Most individual's primary income stream is their job. Your job puts income into your pocket on regular intervals (e.g. Weekly, Bi-Weekly, etc.). Others may be self-employment income (e.g. Barbers, Real Estate Agents, Insurance Agents, etc.). However you make your income, list it on your budget.

This exercise can be a little tricky if you're self-employed as opposed to working a job. A person that works a job usually makes (approximately) the same pay every pay period, unless they work more hours or overtime. Other than that, their pay is pretty consistent. Self-employed individuals, on the other hand, will not make the same exact pay every month. Some months will be more profitable than others. When you earn income in this way, the best thing to do is to create a new budget every time you get paid.

Tracking Your Spending Habits

The next thing that you want to do, to create your budget, is to track your spending habits for at least a month. In today's world, this is extremely simple. You can use your smart phone or tablet to find an app that will enable you to track your daily expenses. However, if you're "old school", just get a little notebook and jot down every item that you purchase. Be sure to record every purchase, no matter how small. Good records are vital to tracking your daily expenses.

During this time, you will find out how much money is going towards legitimate expenses and how much money is going towards wasteful "wants", leisure activities and going out to eat. When I help people with creating their budget, they always try to tell me what they're expenses are from memory. This never works. The reason why it doesn't work is because all people remember are their primary expenses. They never remember their "miscellaneous" expenses and trust me, everyone has them.

For example, when I'm reviewing their budget, they never tell me that they go to the coffee shop and get a coffee every day. That omission may be costing them (approximately) $60 per month, even for a cheap cup of coffee. If they go to Starbucks every day, they may actually be paying $150 per month (approximately $5 per day x 30 days in a month).

Others omit the fact that they purchase breakfast and/or lunch on daily basis. This may be an omission of an additional $200 or more per month. That's why this exercise is so important. It is designed to capture every expense, no matter how large or how small the purchase is. As you practice this exercise, you will learn a lot about yourself. You will learn if you're very frugal or extremely wasteful with your money. However, no matter what you find out about yourself, it's a good thing.

I know that may sound strange, but it's true. If you discover that you waste a lot of money, that information can aid you in repairing that habit. You can't fix a problem that you don't think you have. Once you complete this exercise, you will have irrefutable evidence of your financial habits. After practicing this exercise, most of you will be shocked about how much money you actually waste on things you don't really need.

I have had clients that were amazed at how much money they spend eating out or on purchasing coffee or lottery tickets or smoking. After seeing this, usually most clients can see how they can save more money or actually pay down their debt. As I mentioned earlier, you can use many systems to track your expenses, but I have provided you with a worksheet to get started.

Feel free to use the following "Daily Expense Tracker", create one of your own or find an app on your smartphone that will take care of this for you. No matter how you do it, just get started.

Daily Expense Tracker

Track your daily spending on this worksheet to see exactly where your money is going.

Date	Expense	Amount

List Your Expenses

Now that you've tracked your expenses for a month, it's time to complete your budget. Write down all of your expected expenses for the month. Break them into three categories: fixed expenses, variable expenses and savings.

Your fixed expenses are considered "fixed", because they don't change from month to month. Examples of Fixed include items like your rent or car payment or insurance.

Variable expenses can change from month to month. These expenses include items such as groceries, clothing, eating out, etc. With Variable Expenses, the best thing that you can do is to try and determine an accurate average for these expenses.

In your expense column, you should also include contributions to your retirement accounts, your emergency fund, vacation and other savings goals. You also want to include expenses like a weekly/bi-weekly allowance for yourself, your spouse and children (if applicable) and charitable contributions (e.g. Tithes and Offerings to your local church, United Way, etc.).

It is also important to expense items that you don't necessarily have to pay every month, but that happen occasionally. For example, purchasing clothing, entertainment expenses (e.g. going to the movies or to a play), and unfortunate incidents like car maintenance. Items like car repairs are the things that take you by surprise when they happen. Anything that you don't plan for will always take you by surprise and surprises will always knock your budget out of whack.

What would you do if your car broke down unexpectedly? Well, if you didn't budget for it, you will more than likely have to divert other budgeted dollars towards taking care of this expense. We call that "Robbing Peter to pay Paul". In other words, somebody's not getting paid this month. But, if you budget for these items, you will have money set aside when things like this happen and you won't have to blow your budget to handle the unexpected situation.

Your First Budget Entry....Yourself

As you begin to list your expenses, I'm sure that your first budget entry was probably either your rent or your mortgage payment. And while that is an extremely important budget entry, I still don't believe that it should be your first budget entry.

Your first budget entry and the very first bill that you need to pay is the bill called "YOU". Before you pay anybody else, you need to learn how to pay yourself. Now, you may be saying to yourself, "Why should I do that"? You may be thinking that you have a lot of creditors that you have to pay, so why should you make yourself number one? You have so many debts, so how can you substantiate paying yourself before them? You should, because you're in debt to yourself, you're in debt to your family, and you're indebted to your future. You should pay yourself first, because it's a tragedy to work as hard as you do, on a daily basis, and have nothing to show for it but paid bills. You should pay yourself first, because when you need money, it will be available to you. You should pay yourself, because (by doing it) you're telling yourself and your family that your (and their) future is extremely important to you.

I know that you may have credit card debt, personal loans, utility bills, car notes and other bills that are important, but are they more important than you and your family? I hope your answer is a resounding "No!" In fact, I don't care how important the bill is, it is not more important than your families future. Just like you owe your creditors, you owe yourself. Do I still have to convince you how important it is to pay yourself? I hope not.

How Much Should You Pay Yourself?

The easy answer is, as much as you can. However, since I realize that's not the most practical answer, I will try to help you come up with a number. I always recommend that you should try to save no less than 10% of your gross (before tax) income. If you can save more that would be great. However, if you're not able to save 10%, then save as much as you can. The goal is to get into a habit of saving something.

Most people have a habit of spending everything that they have, but you have to break that pattern. We are creatures of habit and not discipline, but discipline will begin to birth new habits. If you have had a bad habit of spending, you must (through discipline) develop a good habit of saving.

Believe me, you will thank me when you begin to accumulate funds in your bank account. It will feel good to see your balance go up higher and higher. It will feel like a major accomplishment to end this year with some savings in your bank account. So, whatever you have placed as number 1 on your budget, replace it with yourself.

Start an Emergency Fund Account

Now that you've started the habit of paying yourself first, give that money direction. Use it to start building an emergency fund for yourself. This fund should be enough to cover the expenses for minor emergencies (e.g. Car breaks down, refrigerator goes on the blink, etc.) up to major emergencies (e.g. loss of a job). I always say that life happens; it's going to rain, just make sure that you have an umbrella when it does. Just like no one can predict the rain, no one can predict when and where an incident will occur. If you don't have your financial umbrella, you will wind up getting all wet. In other words, if an incident does happen and you don't have the money, where are you going to get it? You will either rob Peter to pay Paul or you will wind up going into debt to take care of the issue.

This is why having an emergency fund is so crucial to your overall financial plan. If you have this money available to you, it won't be a problem for you to take care of the issue without going into debt or ruining your budget. Nothing breaks a person's spirit more than when they begin to make progress and then "life happens". It is what it is. No one can stop life from happening. Again, no one knows when these incidents are going to strike, but that doesn't mean that you shouldn't prepare yourself for it. When you're talking about money, you must always prepare for the unexpected, because it is the unexpected incidents that hurt you financially.

How Much Do I Need in my Emergency Fund?

A fully furnished emergency fund should have enough money available to cover approximately 3 to 6 months of your monthly expenses. For example, if your monthly expenses are $3,000 per month, then you need to save between $9,000 and $18,000 to have a full funded emergency fund. As I mentioned earlier, you can use this fund to help with minor incidents, but the primary purpose of an emergency fund is to protect you against the tragedy of the loss of income.

The truth of the matter is that most people would be completely devastated if they were to lose their job, because the vast majority of people are living paycheck to paycheck. Just think about that for a moment. If someone loses their job, their primary, or maybe only, source of income is gone. If unemployment is available to them, they usually have to wait for several weeks before they receive their first payment. What do they do while they're waiting for that payment? The bills don't stop coming, do they? And let's not forget about the fact that unemployment is only a fraction of what you were being paid, so now you have to learn to live on less money then you were accustomed to making before.

As you can imagine, or may already know, this can be an extremely stressful and desperate time. That's why having a fully funded emergency fund, of 3 to 6 months of expenses, is so vital. If you have this savings available, you won't be as stressed. Your bills will still be paid on time, while you're in the process of looking for another job. You will also have money to last you while you're waiting for your unemployment to come through. You will also have time to look for a better job opportunity.

You don't have to take the first opportunity that comes your way, because you have money to live off for a little while.

Continue Saving and Invest in Your Future

Once you have saved enough money for your emergency fund, that doesn't mean that you should stop saving. Continue the good habit, that you've started, but direct those savings towards other endeavors. For example, start saving to purchase a home or to purchase a rental property. Remember that we discussed assets, in the beginning of this book, now it's time to start acquiring them. People make tons of money in real estate every year. Why not you?

But if real estate isn't your cup of tea, maybe you would prefer saving money to start the business that you always wanted to have. Maybe you would like to invest in the stock market. Bottom line, no matter what you decide to invest in, start building additional streams of income for yourself. Start securing assets that can pay you and your family.

At worst, you create an additional income source for you and your family. At best, maybe it replaces your job and makes you into an entrepreneur. Like I mentioned earlier, find something that interests you and find a way to make it into a business. Save for that business, using the strategies that we just discussed, and start it. That's how you begin to work your way out of your 9 to 5 job. But even if you love your 9 to 5 job, you should always have additional streams of income. Why? What if your job has to lay some people off and you're one of them? Wouldn't it be great to have another income source available for you and your family?

Seven Streams of Income

It is said that most millionaires have at least seven streams of income. These income sources are made up from a combination of Active Income and Passive Income. Active Income is money that you work and are paid for. For example, your 9 to 5 is considered an active income source.

Passive Income is your income that is not tied directly to you physically working for it. For example, the interest and dividends that you earn on stocks and bonds is considered passive income. The idea is to use your savings to begin to build passive income sources. As I mentioned, you probably already have at least one active income source (e.g. your 9 to 5). Now it's time to develop your passive income sources and start your journey towards becoming a millionaire. I'll just give you a few examples and you can do further research to start building.

Retirement Savings

Earlier we discussed retirement savings. Your 401(k) and/or IRA is building a nest egg for you to retire off. In retirement, the goal is that your retirement savings will replace your income and you will be able to live off of it for the rest of your life. The goal is to be able to live off of the interest and the dividends, without having to touch the principal that you saved over the years. Therefore, your retirement savings is going to be an extremely crucial income stream for your future.

Rental Property

As I mentioned a rental property is an excellent way to develop another income stream. If you can purchase a multi-family (3 or 4 or more family) home, your tenants can pay your mortgage, insurance, taxes, water and upkeep, while you live in the house rent free. You may also have some money left over for an additional stream of income. This can free up a ton of money for you. Imagine, if you lived rent free, you'll have more money to save and invest.

Turn a Hobby or an Interest into a Business

If you have a hobby, that you do well, you may be able to turn it into an additional income source. Maybe you like to knit or crotchet. You can make some items and sell them. My mother loves to bake cupcakes, so she started a business selling cupcakes. I love teaching people about finance, so I wrote this book and I am using it as an additional income stream. What do you like to do? Figure that out and find out how to make money doing it.

Now, utilizing the information that you learned in this section use the following "Household Budget Worksheet" to start creating your household budget.

HOUSEHOLD BUDGET WORKSHEET

CATEGORY	MONTHLY BUDGET AMOUNT	MONTHLY ACTUAL AMOUNT	DIFFERENCE
INCOME			
Wages and Bonuses			
Miscellaneous Income			
Income Subtotal			
INCOME TAXES WITHHELD			
Federal Income Tax			
State and Local Income tax			
Social Security/Medicare Tax			
Income Taxes Subtotal			
Spendable Income			
EXPENSES			
Home			
Mortgage or Rent			
Homeowners/Renters Insurance			
Property Taxes			
Home Repairs/Home Improvements			
Association Dues			
UTILITIES			
Electricity			
Water and Sewer			
Natural Gas/Oil			
Telephone (Land Line, Cell)			
FOOD			
Groceries			
CATEGORY	MONTHLY BUDGET AMOUNT	MONTHLY ACTUAL AMOUNT	DIFFERENCE
Eating Out (Lunches, Snacks, Dinner)			
FAMILY OBLIGATIONS			
Child Support			
Alimony			

CATEGORY	MONTHLY BUDGET AMOUNT	MONTHLY ACTUAL AMOUNT	DIFFERENCE
Child Care Expenses			
HEALTH AND MEDICIAL			
Insurance (Medical, Dental, Vision)			
Unreimbursed Medical Expenses, Copays			
Fitness (Yoga, Massage, Gym)			
TRANSPORTATION			
Car Payments			
Gasoline/Oil			
Auto Repairs/Maintenance/Fees			
Auto Insurance			
Other Transportation (Tolls, Bus, Taxi, Subway)			
DEBT PAYMENTS			
Credit Cards			
Student Loans			
Other Loans			
ENTERTAINMENT/RECREATION			
Cable TV/Videos/Movies			
Computer Expense			
Hobbies			
Subscriptions and Dues			
Vacations			
PETS			
Food			
Grooming, Boarding, Vet			
CLOTHING			
New Items			
Dry Cleaning			
INVESTMENTS AND SAVINGS			
401(K) or IRA			
CATEGORY	**MONTHLY BUDGET AMOUNT**	**MONTHLY ACTUAL AMOUNT**	**DIFFERENCE**
Stocks/Bonds/Mutual Funds			
College Fund			
Savings			
Emergency Fund			
MISCELLANEOUS			

Toiletries/ Household Products			
Gifts/Donations			
Grooming (Hair, Make-up, Other)			
Other Miscellaneous Expense			
TOTAL INVESTMENTS AND EXPENSES			
SURPLUS OR SHORTAGE (Spendable Income Minus Total Expenses and Investments)			
ACTION REQUIRED			

Begin to Eliminate any Unnecessary Expenses

Now that your budget is complete, you may notice that you're spending more money than you make. This, as you can imagine, is a problem. When this happens, most people immediately think that they have to make more money and while making more money is an answer and would be nice, that may not be possible at this moment or even necessary. Sometimes the answer is simply eliminating unnecessary expenses. I mentioned earlier, some expenses are not necessary; they're just wants and desires. That's why we wrote down our "Why" earlier. Knowing your "Why" is going to help you eliminate the "Want" expenses.

For example, I already mentioned that a daily coffee habit could cost you $60 (on the low end) to $150 (on the high end). That's a good expense to cut. It can give you an immediate deduction in your budget. I know what you're thinking. You love your coffee. I know you do and so do I. That's why I purchased a coffee machine and became really good at making coffee. In fact, I personally believe that I make a cup of coffee that taste better than any coffee shop, because I make it exactly the way that I like it.

How about cutting out your daily habit of eating out and making your own breakfast and lunch? That could save you more than $200 per month. How about cutting that expensive cell phone off and getting a cheaper phone service? Another way you can cut expenses is by cutting off your cable and just keeping your internet service, and then you can purchase Netflix and watch that. That could save you over $100 per month.

I realize that these cutbacks may seem harsh and extreme, but are these "Wants" more important than your "Why"? If they are, then you don't have a compelling enough "Why". If it is, get rid of these things, so you can accomplish your "Why".

What if I Really Do Need More Money?

After you eliminate all unnecessary expenses, you may discover that you still don't have enough money to pay all of your monthly expenses. That means that you really do need to make more money. Therefore, the question becomes, how do you make more money? In the short term, you can find something that you can sell for a profit. You may have some stuff lying around your house that you can sell in a garage sale or on Ebay or Craigslist. You can make a little extra money delivering pizzas or driving Uber or Lyft, in your spare time. You can also get a certification in an area of interest.

For example, you can become an insurance agent or a Real Estate agent. These commission based opportunities enable you to have the flexibility of being able to work when it's convenient for you. You may also want to tap into your passion and make a side business out of it. For example, if you can cook or bake, you may be able to turn that into a business. Maybe you like to crochet or use your hands to make things. You can use your passions and natural skills and make it a side business for yourself. You may even find out that you can make more money doing your side business, than the money you make at your current job.

Wouldn't that be great if you can turn a hobby into your primary income? It happens every day. If you can utilize your skills to fulfill someone else's need, you can create a business out of it. That's what entrepreneurs do every day. I love to teach people about finance, so I have spent the last 20 years pursuing a career doing what I love. Now, I'm doing what I love on a full time basis. What I always tell people is to discover what you would do for free and make a business out of it. If you can do that, you will never work again. Why? Because when you're doing what you enjoy doing, it never feels like work.

"B" is also for Banking

One of the biggest issues that people have with money is the proper management of their bank accounts. Proper money management requires the utilization of multiple accounts. Each account should be used for specific functions. For example, everyone needs to have a "Primary Checking Account". This is the account where all of your paychecks and other sources of income will be directly deposited. All of the management of your money will start here, then it will be transferred and allocated to your other accounts as necessary. This is the account that you use to pay all of your primary bills (e.g. Mortgage, Rent, Utilities, Car Note, Insurance, Loans, etc.).

The next account that you need is a "Secondary Checking Account". This is the account that you can use for things like your weekly/bi-weekly allowance. Everybody should have this type of account as well, because this is the "unrestricted" account. You can also call this your "Play Money" account. You can spend this money as you see fit. This is the money that you have allotted to yourself to have "fun" with. Your allowance money should be budgeted just like any other expense that you budget. If you're married, you also need a similar account for your spouse. That is her "She Money" or his "He Money" account.

The important thing to remember with this account is that it only gets filled as you get paid. Once you've spent all of the money in this account (e.g. you've had your "fun"), it doesn't get refilled until your next pay period. In other words, the fun is over until the next pay period. With that being said, don't have all of your fun in one day.

The next account, that you should have, is an "Emergency Savings Account". This account is a "dire emergency" account and should be treated as such. I mentioned earlier, you should save (roughly) 3 to 6 month worth of expenses in this account. This account is your "safety net" for the storms of life. This account is your "umbrella" if you have a loss of income for an extended period of time.

After you have a fully funded emergency fund, you can also start an account to save for "Miscellaneous" items. For example, you may want to start a business or you may want to make an investment in the stock market. You may also want to save for a vacation or for a car or for the down payment on a new home. After you save money your emergency fund, you should open another savings account to save for these things as well.

The Envelope System

Clients always ask me how they can stay on top of their budget when they get paid bi-weekly, but some of their bills are due monthly. Unfortunately, most people don't have the discipline to leave money for partial payment of their bills sitting in a checking account. When money just sits there like that, people usually find something to spend it on. A good way to manage this is to use the "Envelope System".

The envelope system is when you withdraw cash, for different bills in your budget, and keep that cash in an envelope until the payment is due. For example, let's say your rent payment is $1,000.00 per month, but you get paid bi-weekly. You can withdraw $500.00 this pay period and then the other $500.00 next pay period. This system allows you to better management larger payments. You should use the envelope system for items that usually hurt your budget.

Balance Your Account by Knowing When Your Payments are Due

If you're going to ensure that you stay on top of making all of your payments on time, it is imperative that you know when your bills are due; particularly the accounts that show up on your credit report. Every 30 days that you're late on paying a debt, your credit score will be negatively affected. In order to make sure that doesn't happen, you have to develop a system of tracking your billing due dates. One way to do this is by placing all of your due dates on your budget worksheet. Another way to do this, in our technologically advanced world, is to receive email reminders from your creditors. If you have online accounts, this should be relatively easy for you to set up. You can also set your accounts up to directly debit your payment from your checking account on the due date. This option requires a little more financial planning, because you have to make sure that the money is in the account on the due date.

The idea is to automate your accounts so you don't lose track of your accounts due dates. You can also use the following "Bill Paying Worksheet" to help you keep track of all of your due dates.

Bill Paying Worksheet

This worksheet is to help you get organized when paying your bills. Take a moment and fill in all of your bills that due within different dates. This worksheet is to assist you in remembering what and when bills are due.

Due Dates – 1st to 7th

Bills to Pay	Due Date	Payment	Bills to Pay	Due Date	Payment
		$			$
		$			$
		$			$
		$			$

Due Dates – 8th to 14th

Bills to Pay	Due Date	Payment	Bills to Pay	Due Date	Payment
		$			$
		$			$
		$			$
		$			$

Due Dates – 15th to 21st

Bills to Pay	Due Date	Payment	Bills to Pay	Due Date	Payment
		$			$
		$			$
		$			$
		$			$

Due Dates – 22nd to 31st

Bills to Pay	Due Date	Payment	Bills to Pay	Due Date	Payment
		$			$
		$			$
		$			$
		$			$

CHAPTER 3

"C" is for Credit

What is Credit?

Credit is money that is borrowed. Usually its money borrowed as a loan used to purchase goods or other services. This "borrowed" money usually comes from a bank or another financial institution. Since this money is a loan, it must be paid back, in a certain amount of time and with interest on the principal amount that was borrowed. Usually, the borrower (you) pays back the creditor (or lender) a minimum agreed upon payment. This payment goes towards paying the principal amount, that was borrowed, and interest of the payment. The payment will continue to be paid until the principal balance is completely paid off. The amount of money that you're eligible to borrow and the interest rate that you will have to pay, on top of the principal amount, is all determined by how good or bad your overall credit history is.

More Valuable than Money?

Whenever I teach on the subject of credit, I always tell my students that having good credit could be more powerful than having money in the bank. I always have many shocked looks when I tell people that, but this statement is not far from the truth. When I purchased my first investment property, I didn't have a dime in the bank; but what I did have was a credit score over 700. Having a good credit score enabled me to get the house without putting any money down. In fact, I was able to negotiate a deal that put over $15,000 in my pocket at closing. That's the power of having excellent credit. You may be saying "I understand that credit is important, but how could it be more powerful than having money in the bank"?

I say this because, during this same time, I was a loan officer and I had a situation that convinced me of this fact. I was working with a couple that came into my office looking to purchase their first home. At the time, they had over $20,000 in savings, but they had extremely poor credit. I must tell you that it was incredibly difficult to get them approved for a mortgage, even though they had money for a down payment and closing costs. The issue (and hindrance) was their poor credit. Now, I found this particularly interesting, because I just purchased a 3 family house, without any money to put down, but I jumped through far less hoops than they had to. The difference was having excellent credit. That is the power of having a great credit score.

Know and Protect your credit

As I just mentioned, your credit can be more valuable than money. People will get more with good credit and no money, than having bad credit with money. Your credit, for all intents and purposes, is like your high school transcript. It literally shows creditors/lenders what kind of a financial student you are. It tells creditors/lenders the likelihood of them being paid back if they were to lend you money. That's why the credit system was established. It was created so creditors could evaluate your payment history. That's why you must know what's on your credit report. You must know and understand your credit score. You must also make sure that the information that's on your report is accurate and free of errors.

Remember, your credit report is the story that your creditors are going to read. Your credit story will determine whether or not you get the loan that you want. It will also determine how much you're going to pay for that loan. It is, therefore, in your best interest that you make sure that they're reading a great story.

Credit is Good, Debt is Bad...

Most people think that credit is bad, but credit isn't bad, DEBT IS. In fact the more available credit you have, the more lending will be in your favor. Now let's talk about the concept of credit to debt ratio. I know this may sound like a complicated concept, but it's really not that difficult. In simple terms, your credit to debt ratio is how much available credit you have as opposed to outstanding debt.

For example, if you have a credit card that has a $1,000 credit limit and you have used $500 of that credit limit, your credit to debt ratio is 50%, because you're using 50% of your available credit limit on that card. So, the more you have in available credit as opposed to outstanding debt, the better your ratio. The better your credit to debt ratio, the more appealing you are to lenders.

In contrast, the more debt you have, as opposed to available credit, the less attractive you look to potential lenders. Why? Because you already have debt that you must pay back. The more debt you have to pay back, the less money you have available to pay another creditor. So, the next obvious question is "What is a good credit to debt ratio?"

A good credit to debt ratio is no more than 30%. For example, if you have $1,000 (in available credit), you never want to use more than $300 (or 30%) of it. Anything higher than that, you run the risk of having your credit score negatively affected. Also, as I just mentioned, you will definitely look less attractive to potential lenders. Ideally, I tell my clients to try not to carry balances from month to month. That's how the interest begins to catch up with you. My golden rule is that, if you can't pay your credit card off by the end of the month, you don't need what you're trying to buy. This one rule will keep you free from the credit trap.

The Credit Trap

So, what is the Credit Trap? The credit trap is my name for the scheme that creditors and lenders use to keep consumers in debt for the rest of their life. For example, have you ever walked into a department store and, as you were about to check out at the register, the person at the register offers you a store credit card? Of course you have. They seem so nice and so kind. In fact, they even tell you that, if you sign up today, you'll get 10% off your purchase. Wow! How kind of them. Definitely not! They're putting out the bait for the trap.

You see, department stores learned, a long time ago, that they make more money off of credit, than they ever made off of any item they sold you in a store. You see most department store credit cards have interest rates of 25%, 30% and higher. What does that mean to the average consumer?

If you bought $500 worth of merchandise at 30% interest and you only paid the minimum payment (which is usually only 4% of the amount or $20 per month), it would take you 58 months to pay off your credit card and it would cost you a total of $929.29 (that's $429.29 of interest).

That's almost double the amount of your actual merchandise. That, my friends, is what I call the credit trap.

Don't fall for it and definitely don't fall into it. Think about this. How many credit card applications have you received in your mailbox this week? Why are companies pushing so hard to give you credit? The simple answer is that they know how much they can make off of you if you sign up for one of their cards. This is how most of us are sucked in to the trap.

How I fell into Credit Trap

I will admit that it happened to me. Yes, I fell into the credit trap. That's why I recognize the trap so well. When I first started college, I was super broke. I was living on campus in a college dorm and was trying to be independent. I was eighteen and I had a job making slightly higher than minimum wage at the time; but, to my amazement, even though I didn't have established credit, the department store gave me a credit card. After securing that credit card, I said to myself "That was pretty easy. I wonder if I can get another one". So, I got another one. And, to my surprise, I got it. Then I borrowed a $1,000 loan from a bank that I frequented. I also took out a loan to purchase a used car. Do you see where I'm going with this?

Before I knew it, I was up to my eyeballs in debt. Making a salary that was slightly higher than minimum wage, there was no way that I could afford to pay for all of this money that I was borrowing. That's the danger of credit. It almost feels like free money. Since you can purchase something without any immediate consequence, it appears to be a great option. I can get what I want NOW! I don't have to wait for it. That appears to be a great option, until the bills start arriving.

At first, I tried my hardest to pay off everything that I purchased; but, I was overcome by the volume of the things that I purchased with credit. After a while, I just gave up. I remember it like it was yesterday. I literally said to myself, "What are they going to do, lock me up"? Please don't judge my ignorance. I was very young and very dumb (LOL!!).

And while they didn't lock me up in the natural, they did lock me up financially. From that moment on, I really struggled to get back on track. It took many years before I was out of the woods and back on my feet. Some of you may have a similar story. The happy ending to this story is that I did get back on my feet and now I'm helping tons of people get back on their feet. Do you realize what that means? It means that if you're in a similar situation, you can also get back on your feet. Maybe you'll be teaching someone else how to get back on their feet in the future. Now, let's talk about how you accomplish that.

Building your Credit Score

Before you can put together a strategy for building your credit, you must first understand how your credit score is evaluated and determined. As I advise my clients, there is a formula to determine your credit score, but it's not one plus one equals two. It's a little more complicated than that. Let me also mention that there are different formulas, for determining your credit score, depending on what company is scoring it. For this book, I'm going to stick with the current industry standard for scoring; which is FICO.

FICO stands for Fair Isaac Company and, as I mentioned, it is the current industry standard for credit scoring. Whenever you're being evaluated (by a creditor) for major purchases (e.g. Mortgages, Car Loans, etc.), this is the scoring system that will be utilized to determine your credit worthiness. As I just mentioned, there are other scoring systems out there. One of the systems, that's gaining popularity, is VantageScore. This is the scoring system that Credit Karma currently uses. However, for the purpose of this book, I'm going to focus on FICO, since it is the industry standard.

What is a Good or Bad Credit Score?

So, what is a good credit score? What is a bad credit score? We're going to take this time to go through the basics so you can understand what type of credit score you have. Your credit score has ranges. These ranges go from 300 to 850. So, as you can imagine, 300 is the absolute worst and 850 is the absolute best. Most people, however, will fall somewhere in between this range. Where you fall, within this range, determines how good or bad your score actually is.

For example, any score that is 549 or lower is considered a "Bad" credit score. From 550 to 649 is considered a "Poor" credit score. Scores ranging from 650 to 699 is considered "Fair". When your credit scores ranges between 700 to 749 you're considered to have a "Good" score and anything 750 or better is considered an excellent credit score.

Remember, your credit score is what's going to determine if you will be extended credit and what your interest rate will be on the credit that you are extended. The better your score, the better your chances of securing credit and the lower your interest rate will be. Now let's take a look and see how your FICO score is calculated.

How are FICO Scores Calculated?

This is the breakdown of how the FICO Score is evaluated. FICO scores are based on several factors:

- 35% on your payment history
- 30% on the amount you currently owe lenders (or how close you are to your credit limits)
- 15% on the length of your credit history
- 10% on the number of new credit accounts you've opened (or applied for).
- 10% on the mix of credit accounts you have (e.g. mortgages, credit cards, installment loans, etc.)

Now let's look at what these percentages mean.

Payment History

It's a no brainer that payment history carries the most weight when it comes to determining your credit score. It counts for 35% of your overall score. Therefore, when trying to establish or re-establish your credit, nothing will assist in this effort more than simply making your payments on time. Late payments cause the most damage to your credit score, so you need to avoid being late at all cost.

Let me provide more clarity about what being late means. Typically, being late means not paying your bill on the due date, but that's not what it means when we talk about your credit report or score. On your credit report, you're not officially late until you're 30 days late. Therefore, even if your due date is the first of every month, you will not be penalized for being late until 30 days after that date.

Once you hit 30 days, you receive a "ding" on your credit. The next "ding" will follow on the 60th day, followed by 90 days and then 120 days. So, every 30 days that you're late, you will receive a "ding" for being late on your credit report. Let me clarify one more thing.

If your payment due date is the 1st, you should pay your bill on the first. Just because you won't be penalized on your credit until your 30 days late, doesn't mean that you should push the envelope. Pay your bill on its due date. Why? Because your creditor will still charge you a late fee if your payment is late. I just wanted to make you aware that your score will not be affected until you hit 30 days.

Account Balance

Account balance is the second weightiest factor that determines your credit score. It accounts for 30% of your overall score. If you recall, I spoke about credit to debt ratio in an earlier chapter. This is where the credit to debt ratio comes in. As I mentioned in that chapter, a good ratio is 30%. Again, that means that you are not using more than 30% of your available credit at a given time.

Creditors want to see that you have low account balances. If you don't, it is proof that your credit is overextended. If you have too much outstanding debt, lenders may not view you as a good credit risk and they won't lend to you. If they do, it will (more than likely) be at higher interest rates. Never forget that the more of a financial risk you are, the more that the lenders are going to charge you in interest or they won't lend to you at all. Also, the higher your credit to debt ratio, the lower your credit score is going to go. Again, the rule of thumb is, keep your outstanding credit below 30% of your available credit.

Length of Credit History

Length of credit history is the length of time that you've had credit. In other words, how long have you been playing the credit game? The longer your credit history, the better your credit score will be. This example will show you how important your length of credit history is and why you should never close a credit card, especially if you've had that card for many years.

I knew someone that had credit score close to 800. That's pretty aweseome, right? Unfortunately, this individual received some horrible advice from a friend of hers. This person advised her that she needed to close some of her credit cards, since she wasn't using them. These are the very credit cards that helped her attain such an excellent credit score in the first place. To her amazement, almost overnight, her credit score plummeted to the 500's and she had no idea how that could possibly happen.

After she discussed this scenario with me, I advised her that the reason why her credit score drastically plummeted was because, by closing those credit cards, she inadvertently erased all of the years of good credit history that she had established with those cards. It was as if those good credit years never happened and like she was just getting started with credit all over again. Again, this is why you should never close a credit card that has a long history. Stop using it, but never close it.

New Credit Accounts and Credit Inquiries

This section pertains to the opening of new accounts. Although it only accounts for 10% of your credit score, doesn't mean that it's a section that can be overlooked. You also don't want to be afraid to open a new account, if it's a good idea to do so. I know many people that are afraid to apply for credit, because they heard that a credit inquiry will ruin their credit score. That's not true. It is true, however, that multiple inquiries in a short period of time can begin to pull your credit score down. That's what you want to avoid.

Mix of Credit Accounts

A good credit mix is having an accumulation of different types of credit. So, let's first talk about the different types of credit accounts. Most accounts usually fall into one of two categories; installment loans or revolving loans. Installment accounts are accounts that have a fixed payment as wells as a fixed period of time for those payments to end. Falling under the installment loan category you have accounts like auto loans, mortgage loans, student loans and other personal loans. For the most part, all of these loans have a fixed amount that you pay every month and they will end after a certain period of time.

The next type of account is a revolving account. Revolving accounts will have different payments each month depending on what your current balance is. Also, you only owe and have to pay back the amount that you've borrowed. As you pay back the borrowed amount, your credit limit goes back up to the original available credit amount.

For example, if you have a credit card that has a balance of $1,000 and you use (or borrow) $300 of the available amount, you only have to pay back the $300 that you borrowed. Also, your available credit is reduced by the amount that you borrowed, so your new credit card balance is $700 ($1,000 - $300 = $700). However, once you pay back the $300, your credit card balance will return to $1,000. That's why they call it a "Revolving" account.

Some examples of revolving accounts include credit cards (e.g. from banks or credit unions, retail stores and gas companies) and Home Equity Lines of Credit. So, a good credit mix, involves a mixture of revolving and installment loans. Therefore, it doesn't look good to have 10 credit cards and that's it. It's a bad credit mix, because you only have revolving accounts and no installment accounts. However, if you have 3 credit cards, a car loan and a student loan, that's considered a good mix. This only accounts for 10% of your overall score, but it's still a factor, so pay attention to your credit mix.

Be Aware of what's on your Credit File

Now that we've discussed your credit score and how it's determined, let's take some time and talk about the credit report itself. First of all, it is of the utmost importance that you become an excellent student of your credit. What I mean by that is that you need to know what's on your credit report at all times and you should be able to read and understand your credit report as well. The wrong time to find out what's on your credit report is when you're trying to make a major purchase.

For example, you go to the car lot and you find the car of your dreams. It's the right make, model, color and the price is right. You negotiate a great deal for yourself and you're sitting down with the sales rep, ready to close. Only one step remains. That's right, they have to pull your credit report. Before you get here, you should already know what's on your credit report. Because if you don't you may wind up getting the surprise of your life. They may pull your credit and tell you that you have been declined. The worst part about it is that they won't even tell you why you've been declined. All they can tell you is that something is on your credit that is causing you to be declined. Now, you really have to check your credit.

This could have been avoided if you would have pulled and reviewed your credit prior to going to the car dealership. I have had tons of clients that have come to me with situations like this. Then, I have to pull their credit for them and review their credit file with them. On top of that, it may take months, if not years, to fix the credit issue itself. That delay can be devastating to you, if you really need a car. Find out early, fix the problem early, and you will have confidence when you're ready to secure that loan.

Getting a Copy of my Credit Report

It's becoming simpler and simpler to get a copy of your credit report in this technologically driven society that we live in. I live in New Jersey and in our state we are able to obtain two free credit reports every year. In most states, you can get at least one free of charge. The main site that I tell people to use is annualcreditreport.com. You can look at all three major credit bureaus (e.g. Experian, Equifax and TransUnion) using their website and, as I mentioned, it is free of charge. This site will allow you to view your credit report and even print and save a copy for your records. The only thing that won't be available to you is your credit score. If you want to view your score, you will have to pay a small fee (approximately $6.00 per credit bureau).

You can also use creditkarma.com. Credit Karma will allow you to view your credit report and your credit score for TransUnion and Equifax. But, as I mentioned in an earlier chapter, Credit Karma doesn't utilize the FICO Scoring Model. They use the VantageScore scoring model. I also stated that FICO was the industry standard, so it's the one that you really want to focus on. That doesn't mean, however, that Credit Karma is useless. It actually serves as a good gauge as to where you are credit-wise. Just know that your FICO may wind up being a little lower. Also, remember that you normally have to pay for your FICO score, but Credit Karma is free. So, it's a good gauge until you're ready to really check your score.

How to Read Your Credit Report

Now that you have your credit report, the next step is to actually understand what you're looking at. Although all three credit reports look different, they all have similar set ups. If you can understand how they're set up, you will have no problem reading all of them. All of your credit reports will be divided into four sections; Identifying Information, Credit History, Public Records and Inquiries. Each section has a different story to tell about your overall credit history. So, let's take a little time to review each section.

Identifying Information

Identifying Information is just what it sounds like. This section contains information that identifies you. This area will include your name (and possible aliases), your current and previous home addresses, your date of birth, telephone numbers, driver's license number and current and previous employers.

As you're reviewing this information, look at it closely to make sure that the information is accurate. It's not unusual for there to be a misspelling of your name or an address that you never lived at. It may be incorrect simply because someone reported it incorrectly. You don't want to be too obsessive about this area though. It doesn't provide any positives or negatives as it related to your credit or your score.

Credit History

The next section is your credit history. Your credit history contains details on each individual account that you have. These individual accounts are also called trade lines. Each account will include the name of the creditor and the account number, which is usually partially blocked out for security purposes. The entry will also include the type of credit that it is (e.g. installment loan or revolving). It will include the total amount of the loan and the high credit limit or highest balance on the card. It will include the current loan and debt balance. It will state what the monthly payment is or the minimum monthly amount. It will also include the current status of the account (open, inactive, closed, paid, etc.). It will show how well you've paid the account (e.g. late or current).

You will also see accounts that have been closed by the consumer, accounts that are charged off or in default and you may see accounts that are in collections. Charged off accounts are accounts that the creditor has given up on. They have contacted the consumer multiple times to get the payment and have been unsuccessful, so they write off the account as a loss. However, just because the creditor has written it off, it doesn't mean that it's gone forever. The next stage is usually collections. A collection account is when a collection agency will buy the charged off account, for pennies on the dollar, and attempt to collect the debt.

Public Records

Public Records is the next section that we're going to discuss. If you see a "Public Record" on your credit report, it's never good news. There is never anything good about having this listed on your report. The information that you will find, on this section of the credit report, include bankruptcies, judgments, repossessions, foreclosures and tax liens.

This information severely hurts your credit and your credit score. An account usually reaches this stage when a court is petitioned to settle the account. For example, if a collection agency can't collect on the debt, they may petition the court to get a judgment against you. If successful, they will be able to garnish your paycheck or take money out of your bank account or seize your federal and state income taxes, to make payment on the debt.

Inquiries

The final section is inquiries. This a list of every company that has asked to see a copy of your credit report. There are two types of inquiries that you need to be aware of. There are "hard inquiries" and "soft inquiries". It's important to know the difference, because some inquiries can actually hurt your credit score.

Soft Inquiries come from creditors that are trying to prescreen you for a credit offer. Have you ever received a pre-approved credit card application in the mail? That came from a "soft inquiry" or a "soft pull". That creditor has pulled a copy of your credit report, without your request or approval. Don't get too upset. Soft inquiries or "soft pulls" don't affect your credit score. It is also a considered a soft pull when you request a copy of your credit report, through companies like annualcreditreport.com or Credit Karma. When you pull a copy of your report, using companies like this, you are also making a soft pull on your credit and you don't have to worry about hurting your credit score.

What you have to worry about are the "Hard Inquiries". Unlike Soft Inquiries, Hard inquiries are initiated by you when you fill out a credit application or a car loan or a mortgage loan, etc. When you apply for a credit card, or a department store card, or an auto loan or a mortgage, the creditor will do a "Hard Pull" on your credit. These pulls can affect your score, especially if you have a lot of them in a short period of time. They also remain on your credit report for two years, although they only negatively affect you for a year.

The Misconception of Hard Pulls

Most people believe that every time there is a Hard Inquiry, your score is negatively affected. That's not true. Also, most people believe that they do major damage, which is also not true. Let's tackle the first misconception.

If you are applying for a loan, that requires shopping around, the credit bureau is sophisticated enough to determine that. For example, if you're buying a car, it's understood that you may go to multiple car lots before making your decision to purchase a car. That means that multiple car lots may make Hard Pulls on your credit. That does not negatively affect your score. Also, if you're purchasing a home, the mortgage company may pull your report several times before you close. This also doesn't negatively affect your credit score. Now, if you go out and apply for 10 credit cards in one day, yes it will affect your score negatively. So, it's important for you to understand the difference.

What type of information will show up on your Credit Report?

Another misconception that people have is the type of information that actually shows up on a credit report, so let's look at what does and doesn't show up on your credit report. Any type of "Line of Credit' will show up on your credit report. For example, Revolving Accounts, such as credit cards, gas cards, department store cards and personal lines of credit.

Also, any type of installment loan will be reported on your credit report. For example, mortgages, student loans, auto loans, personal and business loans. You will also see delinquent accounts that haven't been paid as of yet. These are generally accounts that have gone into collections. These accounts include unpaid utility bills, cell phone bills, medical bills, library fees and bank overdrafts. Finally, you will see accounts that have become lawsuits that have been filed as an unpaid debt.

What type of information WON'T show up on your Credit Report?

Now that we've discussed what will show up on your credit report, let's discuss what won't show up on your report. You will not see bank accounts or debit cards. You will not see your "on time" rent payments. You will not see "on time" payments made to your medical bills, phone/cell bills, utility bills or your cable bills. These accounts will only be reported on your credit if you default on them and they go into collections. Yes, I agree, this is extremely unfair, but this is the way that the current credit reporting system works. What's important is that you know what will be on your credit report and since you know, you can do something about it.

Correcting Errors found on your Credit Report

One of the main reasons to stay on top of your credit is to make sure that there are not any errors contained in it. Yes, there is a chance that you will pull your credit report and find that some of the information is not accurate. You may find some outdated information on your credit report. You may find a debt that you've already paid, lingering on your credit report. You may even find an account that was never yours in the first place.

I remember working with a young man, who was interested in purchasing a car. He decided to sit down with me and take a look at his credit report before going to the car dealer (bravo to that young man). This proved to be an extremely wise decision for this young man. He sat in my chair, confident that his credit score was excellent. To his amazement, his credit score was (for the lack of a better phrase) in the toilet. He couldn't believe his eyes when he saw multiple collection accounts for medical bills. What amazed him the most was the fact that he was very healthy and had never been to any of the doctors listed on his credit report.

As we began to dig further, we discovered that all of those medical bills actually belonged to his father. You see, he and his father shared the same name and the physician made the mistake of charging his father's debt to him. This had gone on for about five years before we caught it. I learned two lessons that day. The first was, always check your credit report for accuracy. The second was, if I ever have a son, never name my son after me (LOL!!!).

With that being said, if you find a mistake on your credit report, you have the right to dispute it with the credit bureau that you found the error with. The credit bureau (by law) has to investigate the debt by contacting the creditor(s). The creditor(s) then has 30 days to respond to the dispute. If they do not respond to the dispute, or they can't prove that the debt actually belongs to you, they have to remove the inaccurate information from your credit file. The easiest way to make your dispute is to go to annulacreditreport.com and make an online dispute. You can also make your dispute in writing.

Repairing your credit

Now that you have reviewed your credit report for inaccuracies, you now know what you're working with. Now it's time to start working on eliminating the debt and repairing your credit. The first step, if you are currently behind on payments, is to contact your creditors. Preferably not after months and months of extremely harassing phone calls, but as soon as you realize that you will have a problem with making your payments. However, before you contact them, make sure that you determine how much you can pay them to settle the debt. This is where the power of your budget will come into play. Make sure that you negotiate an amount that you can handle. Remember, you're calling your creditor to negotiate. Make sure that you can make good on the arrangement.

Also, remember that this is a negotiation. That means that no amount, that you offer, is out of the question, so never offer the full amount. Lowball them and make them counter offer. Your goal is to get the best deal possible. Don't let your creditor intimidate you. They are not being paid anything right now and something is better than nothing. Don't be afraid to tell them your "sob story". At the end of the day, they all have room to negotiate and if the person that you're speaking with doesn't have any authority to negotiate, ask for their supervisor and start the negotiation process over again.

Get any agreement in writing

Once you verbally negotiate a payment arrangement, with a creditor, make sure that you request that they send you a letter confirming the negotiated terms. Having it in writing is your defense against them changing their mind (after you sent the payment), lost records, new management being more aggressive, or any number of other things that could go wrong with the agreement. Once you pay off your debt, make sure that you get a settlement letter and send a copy of it to the credit bureaus so they can update your credit file. Then make sure that you check with the credit bureaus to ensure they have updated the record.

How to Establish and Re-establishing Your Credit

One of the best ways to establish or re-establish your credit is by applying for a secured credit card. I usually work with two types of clients. The first type of client has bad credit and needs to re-establish. The other type of client has no credit and needs to establish credit. They are both (almost) in the same position credit-wise. Most people don't realize this, but having no credit is almost as bad as having bad credit. Why? Because, creditors use the credit bureaus to assess the risk of lending money to borrowers. When you have no credit history, creditors are taking almost the same risk on you as they would if you had bad credit. They really don't have any information to determine the likelihood of you paying them back. That's why most new borrowers will be denied unsecured credit cards.

Therefore, the best option for new borrowers, as well as borrowers with bad credit, is to start off with a secured credit card. This involves depositing some amount of money (usually about $300.00) with a bank. The amount you deposit will represent your credit limit. This is where most people get confused with secured credit cards and debit cards. With secured credit cards, you are not actually spending the money that you deposit. Your deposit is put into a CD type of account and is used only as collateral, in the event that you don't pay the lender back. As long as you make your payments on time, that money will never be touched. In fact, usually (after about a year) your deposit will be refunded to you, with interest, and your secured card will become an unsecured credit card.

Also, if you keep a good financial record the bank is likely to raise your credit limit over time. Let me also mention this, secured credit cards work just like unsecured credit cards. Just like unsecured credit cards, they are reported to the credit bureaus. There is no indicator on your credit report that it's a secured credit card either. Only you and the bank know that it is a secured credit card. Also, when you're looking for a secured credit card, don't shop around too much as a sudden increase in inquiries of your credit history can actually lower your credit score. The best place to start with is a bank that you already frequent. If you already have a checking or savings account with them, it makes since to get a credit card with them as well.

Use an old Credit Card

If you already have a credit card, that you haven't used in a while, it would be a good idea to use that card to help you re-establish your credit. The good news is that the older your credit history, the better. You can use the card to make a small purchase from time to time and pay off the balance in full when you get your monthly statement.

Make Payments on Time

I realize that this probably goes without saying, but one of the best things you can do, to improve your credit score, is to simply make your payments on time. The quickest way to stop your momentum, of building your credit, will be a missed or late payment. One of the best things that you can do to avoid this is by setting up automatic payments. In fact, the more you automate the better. It can be a huge task to try to remember every single due date, especially if you have multiple accounts that you have to manage.

If automation is not a possibility for you, write down all of your due dates for all of your debts and look at it regularly. At least make a habit of checking it on your pay days. Make sure that you pay at least the minimum payment. Also, remember that you have 30 days before the debt is reported as a late payment to the credit bureau. Now, that's not an excuse to pay late, it's just a cushion in the event that you run late for an unseen reason.

Never max out your credit cards

Another thing that will hinder your progress in growing your credit score is maxing out your credit cards. Never do this. I mentioned this earlier in the book, but do not forget that the goal is to get your credit-to-debt ratio below 30%. As long as your credit card is over that 30% mark, you will find it more difficult to raise your credit score, even if you're paying your bill on time. You will have to battle with this until you pay off your debt, but this is just a reminder to work towards this goal. Once you establish your goal, of being under 30%, work to never allow it to get over 30% again.

Make the Collection Accounts a Priority

Your first focus in re-establishing your credit is dealing with those pesky collection accounts. Collection accounts only hurt your credit and will continue to hurt your credit until they're either paid off or disputed and removed. So, make collection accounts a priority as you work towards rebuilding your credit. Get rid of them as soon as possible. The sooner you get rid of them, the sooner you will start seeing improvement on your credit reports.

Before you pay a Collection Agency

I know that many of you will think that I'm crazy for saying this, but you may not have to pay that collection agency after all. The first thing that you need to realize is that (by law), you don't owe the collection agency any money. I realize that statement sounded even crazier than the first, but think about this. Did you take out a credit card or a personal loan with the collection agency? I'm assuming your answer is an emphatic "NO". You owed the creditor that originally extended the credit to you. Technically speaking, you don't legally owe the collection agency until they validate the debt. Well, then how do they go about validating the debt?

In order to validate the debt, they must have proof, from the original creditor, that you signed a contract with their company. My question to you is how many loans have you actually signed for, unless it was for a car note or a mortgage? Probably none, right? That is the collection agencies first problem. There is really no record, other than the creditor's word, that you actually owed them anything. Furthermore, when the original creditor couldn't collect the debt from you, they wrote the debt off on their taxes. That's the collection agencies second problem. So, what do you do?

Dispute the debt with the credit bureau. By law, the credit bureaus have 30 days to verify, with the collection agency, that the debt actually belongs to you and that they have validated it. If they can't, then the credit bureau must remove it from your credit report. Always try that first. If that doesn't work, then send a certified letter to the collection agency, asking them to validate the debt. Again, they must have proof of a signed contract with the original lender. In almost every instance, they will not be able to produce those records. And, even if you do owe them the money, they can't collect it, because they can't prove that you do. Using this method, you can usually eliminate the debt.

Take out a personal loan

I used this tactic to rebuild my credit. I took out a personal loan, for $1,000, with my bank. Then I opened a checking account with the same bank and deposited the $1,000 loan. I, then, allowed them to directly debit the monthly payments out of that account every month, when the payment was due. So, the money that I borrowed was used to pay back the loan itself. For an entire year I had on time monthly payments reported to the credit bureau, without me even thinking about it.

Use, don't abuse, your credit cards

This is probably one of the most important lessons that you can learn about your credit. Credit is to be used, not abused. It is to be used to establish good credit, not to fund a lifestyle. Your credit card is not your emergency fund. As we discussed earlier, it is important to establish a cash emergency fund for emergency situations. With that being said, my rule of thumb is, if you can't pay off your balance by the end of the month, you don't need to buy whatever it is that you're trying to buy.

So, your card should not be utilized to buy "big ticket" items like TV's. Remember, your credit cards have one purpose. That is, to establish a good payment history, so that lenders can see that you're responsible. You, therefore, want to purchase things that you would normally buy with cash and then pay off your bill when it comes. For example, buy your groceries on your credit card. You have to eat and you would normally pay cash for that purchase. Set the cash to the side and pay the debt off when the bill comes. If you drive, use your credit card for gas. Then pay it off. If you use public transportation, buy your bus card or your rail pass with your credit card. When the bills comes, pay it completely off. This is how you establish a credit card history and build up your credit, without going into debt.

Request a credit line increase

After you establish (or re-establish) a good credit history, you can contact those credit card companies and request that they give you a credit limit increase. The benefit of this is that increasing your credit will also improve your credit-to-debt ratio, by giving you more available credit. You can try to do this every 6 months to a year, but you shouldn't try to make more requests than that. Remember, whenever you request a credit line increase, it usually triggers a hard pull to your credit. You want to make sure that you limit the hard pulls to your credit, because that can negatively affect your credit score if you have too many of them.

Never close credit accounts

I mentioned this before, but I will mention this again. Do no close your credit card accounts. You can cut them up, if you have to, but never close them. As I mentioned before, when you close credit accounts it erases all of the credit history of that account. This could result in a lower credit score, because you could potentially be erasing years of positive credit history.

Once you've built your credit, begin to use it to your advantage

This is just a quick story on what's available for you once you have good credit. I'm sure that you have heard of credit cards that offer rewards, right? Well, now I'm going to teach you how to use them to your advantage.

Did you know that you can make the credit card companies pay you to use their card? No, this is not a hoax. It's really true! Very few people take advantage of it, because they're too busy swimming in credit card debt to do so. That's what the credit card company is banking on, but this is how you can win.

I have a friend that charges all of their monthly expenses on their credit card. She pays her mortgage, her food, gas and everything else on her credit card. These, of course, are expenses that she would normally pay with cash, but she pays them with her credit card so she can get the reward points. Soon as the bill comes, she pays the bill off in full. That way, she doesn't get caught up with paying the interest on the card.

At the end of every year, she has a ton of reward points that she can exchange for cash, travel or gifts. Mind you, she also has no credit card debt, because she only purchases things that she intended to pay cash for in the first place. She also has a credit score in the high 700's. That is how you begin to win at the credit game my friend. You begin to flip it on the credit card companies and make them pay you. We call that #CREDITGOALS.

CHAPTER 4

"D" is for Debt Elimination

In the previous section on Credit, I mentioned that Credit was good but it was the Debt that was problem. Debt is the number one assassinator of your financial dreams. Because of debt, people find it difficult, if not impossible, to save money. Monthly payments to credit card bills, auto loans, student loans and personal loans (quite literally) suck up most (if not all) of people's disposable income. This income could be used for savings and investing, but it's going towards monthly payments that seem like they will never end. That's why it's imperative that you have a systematic program to deal with your current debt situation. If you don't, you may never reach financial independence.

The good news is that you've already taken the first steps, in the previous chapters. Hopefully you've completed your budget worksheet and you have taken a look at your credit report. These two steps will be vital in you working towards eliminating your debt.

If you've looked at your credit, you now know what debts you must pay. If you've completed your budget and eliminated unnecessary expenses, you should have freed up some money to save and to pay your debt with. Once you've done these two things, you can now put together a plan to pay off your current debt. My personal recommendation is utilize the debt snowball method to work towards eliminating your current debt.

Start the Debt Snowball Rolling

There are many different methods that people use to pay off their debt. My personal favorite is the "Debt Snowball Method". In order for this method to work to its fullest potential, you have to find an extra $100.00 to $200.00 (per month) in order to create your "Debt Snowball" and get it to start rolling. If you haven't found this extra money, go back to the budgeting section and figure out how to eliminate some unnecessary expenses, that will add up to this amount. Or, you can work towards building an additional income source in order to secure this money. So, how does it work?

First, make sure that you pay the minimum payments on all debts to stay current. Next, find that additional $100.00 to $200.00 a month, to begin the debt snowball rolling. Then, list your debts from smallest to largest, and begin paying off the smallest debt first. Add the $100.00 to $200.00 (additional payment) to the minimum payment on your smallest debt. This will get your debt snowball rolling.

Once the first debt is paid off, apply the minimum payment of the first debt to the minimum payment of the second debt, and then add the $200.00 from your debt snowball as well. Once the second debt is paid off, apply the minimum payment of debts one and two, plus the $200.00, to the minimum payment of debt number three. Continue this process until all subsequent debts are paid off. That's how you utilize the Debt Snowball Method to get out of debt.

Depending on how much debt you're in, this process could take several months or several years. The key is to just stick with it. Don't give up until all of your debts are paid off. Once you do that, all of those monthly payments will be available to you for savings and investment purposes. That's worth it, isn't it?

Other Strategies for Paying Off Debt

The Power of Splitting your Payments

The split-payment method is a very simple, but extremely powerful strategy to help pay your debt off quicker. You simply split your monthly payments and make a half payment every two weeks. I know that sounds simple, and it is, but it works wonders for paying off debt. Paying your debt this way actually has three primary benefits.

First, by paying your debt this way, you will automatically make one extra payment per year. If you pay once a month, you will only make 12 payments; but, if you pay bi-weekly, you will make 26 half payments, which equals 13 full payments.

Second, you will lower the principle balance of your loan by 26 (26 payments in a year), instead of 12 payments if you were to continue paying your debt monthly. This is important, because it helps to slow down the rate of interest on the loan. You see, when you borrow money, it's really the interest that hurts you. The interest is what slows you down while you're trying to pay off the principle balance of the loan. The longer gap you have between payments, the more interest is able to accrue on the loan. That's why making 26 payments, instead of 12 payments, help you pay the debt off faster.

The third benefit is that, since most people receive their income on a bi-weekly basis, it will help you manage your payments more efficiently. If you pay all of your debt in this way, you will not have to be as concerned about when the due date of the payment is. This makes it much easier to budget your money more effectively.

Apply your Raises to your Debt or Savings

I always advise my clients that just because their income increases doesn't mean that their expenses have to increase as well. If you receive a raise this year, instead of finding new ways to spend the money, apply the increase to your debt and pay it off faster. You lived without the increase for the last year, so you can continue to live without it as you pay off your debt.

Remember, financial independence is a choice. You make a choice to be financially independent every time you say "No" to a want or a desire. Every time you choose to save money or pay off debt, instead of purchasing something that won't further your financial goals, you make a choice to be prosperous.

So, once you get that raise, just act like you didn't receive it. Take it and use it to make you financially free. Add it to your "Debt Snow Ball" to make it bigger and to get it rolling faster. Once you've paid off your debt, you now have this additional income to apply to savings and investing for your future.

If you've already saved your emergency fund, it's time to maximize your investments. Use this additional money to make more money. The idea is to get to your "wealthy place" as fast as you can. Once you reach this place, you can enjoy the fruits your labor.

Consider Financial Counseling

If you're finding it difficult to determine how to start or even where to start, it may be a good idea for you to speak with a financial counselor. Sometimes it helps to have an impartial set of eyes helping you look at your finances, as you consider making some adjustments to the way you spend your money. I wish I had a dime for every person that told me that they already had a budget and that they didn't think they required my assistance. I would definitely be a multi-millionaire right now. You see, a budget doesn't just consist of a list of income and expenses on a piece of paper or a spreadsheet. That is what most people mean when they say "I have a budget". The purpose of the budget is to analyze where you're at and then make changes so you can arrive where you want to be.

Oftentimes, that's where my services as a financial advisor are most needed. I'm here to tell you that you're paying too much for your car insurance. I'm here to tell you that you need to cut off that expensive cable package. My job is to let you know that there are less expensive cell phone options. It's a difficult job, but somebody has to do it (LOL!!!).

Now that you have the tools to become debt free and financially independent, it's time to for you to use them. Go back over this book (multiple times) and make sure that you apply the methods of each section to your personal financial situation. You're on your way to financial independence. Stick with it and you will get there. I wish you much success.

FOR SPEAKING ENGAGEMENTS

CONTACT ME AT:

EMAIL: MYMONEYONMYSTREET@GMAIL.COM

FACEBOOK: https://www.facebook.com/groups/moneyonmystreet/